Lyris

Poems and Selections by Lyris Hyatt

Edited with commentary
by Vera P. Glenn

Published by
the Academy of the New Church
Bryn Athyn, Pennsylvania
United States of America

700 copies 1988

Printed by
General Church Press
Bryn Athyn, Pennsylvania

ISBN 0-910557-21-7

Preface

By happy accident one afternoon in mid-June 1987, I met Janna Odhner at the Bryn Athyn Swim Club. We had already discussed at an earlier time the possibility of working together on making a selection of Lyris's poems to be published. Now Janna told me that she was returning to Bread Loaf to complete work for her master's degree and would have no time for the project until the fall.

When I offered to read over the poems while she was away and pick out those I specially liked, she gladly accepted. Two days later she brought to my door a cardboard file of Lyris's poems and a boxful of folders with her letters and other material. I'm sure Janna had no more intention of shifting the project entirely from her house to mine than I did of undertaking it alone, but from the moment I began to delve into the poems and memorabilia I was caught up.

All through the hot summer I worked—with delight—reading poems, tracing their inception and progress, making notes, and fitting together the artistic life of a poet. It was an exciting experience. For the first time I felt the lure of scholarship in pursuing primary source material, in deciphering another's yet unexplored work, and adding to it my own thoughts and affectionate response.

So the project grew under my hand from a selection of poems to a kind of biography.

I was fortunate to have known Lyris in a variety of roles. As a pupil in the Girls School, 1950-1954, I had four years of English with Miss Lyris. I learned to know my teacher as a lover of words and of the way they had been put together by great writers, and of the way they could be put together, even by novices, to express the true and the good. When I returned to teach in the Girls School, after college, I began to know Lyris as a colleague. From then on she was Lyris, expecting no deference and giving no advice, unless asked for it. She was an individual. Even though you loved the same literature and worked for the same standards in written work, you were an individual too, your approach and her approach would, and should, be different.

In the summer of 1963 we went together on a trip to England, a six-weeks tour sponsored by the National Council of Teachers of English. I got to know Lyris in a new way, as a traveling companion. On tour there are always ups and downs, and in that summer it rained a lot. We were counting the sunshine in minutes. I came to appreciate Lyris's sense of humor. By the end of the tour we may have been the only two still speaking to each other cheerfully. Although we did many things together, I found that Lyris liked to make discoveries on her own. She walked faster than I did, ranging out ahead like an Irish setter nosing out things. Then she would circle back to tell me about them, pointing out what I shouldn't miss.

Lyris and I are both alumnae of the Bread Loaf School of English. She was already a graduate before she persuaded me to go there, but we were both there in the summer of 1965 when Lyris returned to take a course in writing poetry with the poet, John Frederick Nims. She had given me a summer to find my own way before she came back. This thoughtfulness was typical of Lyris. She never hovered. Even though she wanted others to be close to her by sharing the things she loved, she always gave us our own space.

Looking back down the years of our acquaintanceship, perhaps especially to the summer of 1965, which was such a productive time for Lyris in her writing, I'm astonished that I was so unaware of her poetry. I never once asked to read any of the poems that she was working on. Lyris's sister Morna said that she felt sorry that the family had paid so little attention to Lyris's poetry. So perhaps the same unawareness of Lyris as a poet was true of others too. Only a few poems were published during her lifetime—one as a hymn with the best line altered, according to Lyris. There were the Advent poems that came as her Christmas message to her friends for more than ten years, but they tended to get lost in the shuffle of other cards.

Lyris in her role as poet was, thus, largely unfamiliar to me. Having known so many of the same people and shared similar experiences helped me greatly in understanding something of what Lyris was trying to do and say in her poetry. But the person I found there was a woman I had never known well before. In spite of a large family, scores of students, and some good friends, Lyris was essentially alone. In writing poems was her inner life. Discovering this life was, for me, a tremendous privilege.

VPG

Acknowledgments

For her enthusiastic support, encouraging my efforts and feeding me useful material, also for securing permission to reprint the poems published elsewhere, and for proofreading and catching errors in my text, I'd like to warmly thank Morna Hyatt.

For her useful collaboration in getting this book in print, but especially for her artistic contribution, many thanks to Martha Gyllenhaal.

Table of Contents

Pictures

Part I
The English Teacher

Winters aren't what they used to be.
~~When~~
What used to get cold wasn't all of me,
But only my hands and nose & feet

Winters are what they have always been,
Detriment & benefit
~~Ice & slush and salt & grit~~
~~Frost outside but fires within~~
Cold and warmth both genuine
Exasperating & exquisite

Winters are what they have always been, 2/12/61
Detriment and benefit.
Pristine snow & dirty grit
Alternate their discipline,
~~Flake and flaw both genuine~~
Flaw & flake both genuine,
Exasperating & exquisite

Lyris was a student and a teacher. Thirty-four years she served the Academy as a teacher of English literature and composition, serving for a time as head of the English department. She dedicated herself to this useful career in the Church, passing on to an entire generation of students the love of literature and poetry she felt so deeply and cultivated throughout her lifetime. She made her students aware of the power of language and the careful craftsmanship required to use it well.

from the Resurrection Address given December 10, 1986
by the Rev. Kurt Asplundh

Over the years Lyris received many expressions of appreciation for what she had given to her students. Some of them came in letters and others were spoken. Girls continued to ask her advice about what to read, and to send their poems for her comments even after her retirement. Although most of the young writers that Lyris encouraged never got as far as publishing, still her influence on their affections was great.

It is certain that many more people think of Lyris as an English teacher rather than a poet, and yet here is evidence to show that she combined these talents. This is an early poem written for students about learning to love poetry. It is a lilting sonnet.

A Note About Dating the Poems

The dates given at the end of the poems are taken from the master list Lyris made, or else from the copy of the poem used in this book, if there was a discrepancy. Sometimes there are two dates, one when the poem was first written and another for the date it was revised. The question marks are always those of the poet.

1

I make a wager with you here today
That if you go on reading poetry
With open mind to seek and see the way
The poet chooses what he'll have you see
And feel, iambic meter soon or late
Will grow on you and come to give delight.
No more will you count out or estimate
Iambic feet in fives you're told are "right";
You'll sense it in your brain or in your bones
(Or where it is we keep the things we find)
And read beyond the separate bars and tones
To hear the song the poet had in mind.
Remember, still, that though form may be clever,
The form alone is not a poem—ever.

1952-3?

Lyris once wrote to a friend and fellow teacher:

> *I'd love to hear more about your teaching. I frequently get depressed about what an inferior job I do at it, but then something encouraging turns up. I don't know very much even now, but I think part of the trouble is that I am horrified that the girls don't know something that I think is important until I look back and find that I didn't learn it until long after high school.*

Here is another delightful teaching sonnet about what poetry is and how to distinguish it from prose.

2

"What do you mean by *poetry*?" you ask.
"What do you mean by saying this is prose—
Yet this a well-wrought poem?" You set a task
I used to set once too. Your words are those
We used to ask of those we thought would know—
Of those who'd surely know and have the words
To tell us why some special sounds will flow
Like cream or catch our hearts like singing birds.
Oh yes, they'd try; they'd grope, and then they'd fail;
And I shall fail you now as they failed then.
Words make a poem, yet words are poor and pale
To tell what poems really are. For when
You try to touch a wild bird's fluttering wing.
It never chooses just that time to sing.

1955?

Dedicated to the Junior Girls is a delightful verse in ballad style to demonstrate how to write a ballad.

Lyris had a theory that if information were put into a memorable form it would stick in your mind. She had all kinds of little games and gimmicks for remembering tricky spelling or punctuation.

For years the Junior class was Lyris's class. She was their advisor, chaperoning for dances and meetings, bolstering the girls' class president, trying to make being a Junior girl a happy experience. This was the year of her favorite course, English Language and Literature, where every girl learned by heart the first lines of Chaucer's Prologue to the *Canterbury Tales*, and produced a personal poetry anthology.

Dedicated to the Junior Girls

(Without whose inspiration this would never have been written.)

There was a happy Junior class,
But now it's full of woe;
If in their English they would pass,
The ballad they must know.

* * *

A ballad has a rhyming scheme;
It has four lines per verse.
It shouldn't make you want to scream—
It really might be worse.

A B C B's the rhyming scheme—
At least the easy one,
But others too are possible,
And all of them are fun.

The lines are measured out in feet.
The accents don't ignore.
The second line and fourth have three;
The other two need four.

The ballad always tells a tale—
At least it usually does;
And when you write one for yourself,
You really get a buzz.

* * *

There is a clever Junior class,
And now it's having fun.
The girls write ballads in a flash.
They're passing—every one!

Again a poem about writing—a palatable way to get across some essentials about good writing.

Lyris notes at the end of the poem, *[This was] advice composed after reading a set of high school English themes.*

4

Choose your theme and give the facts;
If you do a good job, your *reader* reacts.

If your facts are clear
And your feeling is real,
You don't have to tell him
Just how he should feel.

He'll feel the way
You want him to;
He'll feel at once
What you say is true.

Don't say something's "greatest"
Or say that it's "rot,"
For nine times in ten
We'll know that it's not.

If the snowfall is lovely,
Don't rave on and gush;
Make us see what it *looks* like,
Make *us* sense the hush.

It's best not to shout
That the scene that you saw
Is just too romantic
For mortal to draw;

Your reader would like
To be given the chance
To see for himself
That the scene has romance.

If your story is touching,
Don't insist that it's so;
Just make it seem touching
And then let it go.

September 17, 1970

It isn't easy to be an English teacher, particularly when it comes to grading and commenting on student writing. So much is neither right nor wrong, but a matter of ear and taste. And amateur writers are very defensive of their own.

A verse which Lyris wrote for *The Academian*, printed in the May 20, 1955 issue, ends with these lines:

Oh please concur

with me. I close my eyes

To much that I despise.

I simply can't praise all.

But your reproachful eyes

Will haunt me down the hall.

Lyris Hyatt
from "The Critic and the Criticized"
With apologies to W.W. Gibson

Lyris was sensitive to her students' feelings as the poem **Admission** shows. She didn't want to be known as a mean teacher. But in working with young people there is much that has to be said and corrected, and any good teacher cares more about learning than being liked.

Lyris wanted the girls to do well, to *earn* good grades, not just be handed a placebo. She set high standards, and when they were met she was as enthusiastic about the results as the student.

5
Admission

The chance word
said, heard.

Just what she needed
though scarcely heeded—

or so I thought
till something caught

her lip and throat.
...What antidote?

Oh, I didn't mean....
But can't you see....
Just give me credit....

Yet the word *was* mean,
admittedly.
And I had said it.

1963

6
Mean Teacher

When weaklings call her mean, she doesn't mind;
Not that she does not care to be thought kind,
But thinks she just can't spare the time it takes
From serving hearty meals to hand out cakes.

March 25, 1959

7

Audio-visual Aids

Hearing is synonym for heeding
No more than seeing words is reading.
To heed or read, we deaf and blind
Must learn by heart to pay full mind.

November 11, 1958

First published in *The Humanist*, 1962, No.2&3, p.71

One of the things Lyris used to say about teaching was: *I took this job because I like to talk.*

She said about herself (probably in answer to a question on the Personal Evaluation of the 1972 application for Accreditation by the Middle States Association):

> *I am somewhat bothered by the fact that I tend to talk pretty much about myself anyway—personal experiences, enjoyments, and the like—and that too many "I" messages make me sound as if my concerns matter more than they really should for the students. Children shouldn't "brush their teeth for Mama" but because doing so is useful. Students shouldn't do their work just to please me but because it is a means to their being or becoming more useful. It bothers me that even some of the older girls seem to fail to recognize the difference between pleasing Miss Lyris because she is "getting what she wants" and pleasing her because they are getting and doing what Miss Lyris thinks and feels is really good for them.*

The allusion in **Verbose** to knowing a handsaw from a hawk comes from *Hamlet*, where the prince is explaining that he is truly rational and only talks wildly when it suits him.

8

Verbose

A word to the wise is said to suffice
And brevity's deemed the soul of wit.
I used to try to be quite concise
But now I've changed my style a bit:
I know a handsaw from a hawk,
And anyhow, I like to talk

January 19, 1962

Part II
Verses for Occasions

Lyris was a teacher, but she was also a loving family member, a friend, a colleague, and an involved person in the community. So, over the years she wrote many, many occasional verses. Most are fun and rollicking, some have a serious side to them, many of them are really good, and all are clever. A sample of them is included here as they represent an aspect of Lyris that might be called the social poet.

Occasional Verse is a bit of doggerel expressing the predicament of those who cleverly turn out verses for occasions like birthdays and anniversaries, and so many times get prodded to produce a poem for "the occasion" even when there isn't much inspiration.

9

Occasional Verse

The certainty of mild success
In impulse writing, speech, or dress
Can't counteract my wild despair
when I haven't a thing to say or wear.
With mind and wardrobe both a mess
The wise one would stay home, I guess,
But dialog's better than monolog:
I put out doggerel if I can't put on dog.

July 8, 1963

Morna is the next sister down from Lyris, who was the oldest of the large family. The sisters always had different interests, but shared a love of the essentials: the Church, the Academy, and teaching. They also shared space, each having a bedroom on the third floor of the Hyatt house on Alnwick Road. They are the two doting aunts of **Two Aunts and the Two-year-old.** Although each insisted on her own identity, they were often named together, "Lyris and Morna," as if they were twins.

Morna was born February 22, the same day and month as George Washington, (but not the same year). This was a verse written for her birthday in 1961.

10

M is for the Math she loves of course
O is for the Overtime she works
R is for the Rules she must enforce
N is for the Needs she never shirks
A is for Adventures she won't scorn...Uh...
Put them all together: they spell MORNA,
The personage whom little ever irks,
The principal perforce of great resource.

February 22, 1961

Andrew Doering was a much loved and respected medical doctor in the Bryn Athyn community and environs for many years. For his birthday in 1963 Lyris paid him this light-hearted, but warm tribute.

Notice the variety of rhymes on his name. She must have had a good time with this one.

11

Almost born, or ninety nearing—
Keep in touch with Dr. Doering.

Children need the best of rearing:
Get the word from Dr. Doering.

Oil for soothing, salve for smearing—
Get advice from Dr. Doering.

Spots or blotch or rash appearing?
Report at once to Dr. Doering.

Fever rising, persevering—
Lose no time—call Dr. Doering.

The fever's down, the tongue is clearing—
Check in once more with Dr. Doering

Small boy bruised while buccaneering—
Should you phone for Dr. Doering?

Wounded by accidental spearing—
Get on the phone for Dr. Doering.

Bikes collide in wild careering—
Send out a call for Dr. Doering.

The cast is tight, needs cutting, shearing—
It needs the touch of Dr. Doering.

Check the symptoms, doubting, fearing—
Allay your fears, phone Dr. Doering.

A sled goes smash from reckless steering—
Find a phone—dial Dr. Doering.

Loss of voice or loss of hearing?
Better go see Dr. Doering.

A virus all your plans are queering—
Get a shot from Dr. Doering.

Your previous vim is disappearing—
Get more shots from Dr. Doering.

Your ear is sore from a too-tight earring—
Refrain from calling Dr. Doering.

He's tired of ills—he must need cheering—
Let's go call on Dr. Doering.

We're certainly glad that he is handy.
A very Happy Birthday, Andy!

January 16, 1963

The (Nothing) in the first line of the next poem refers to the fact that Kenneth Rose has no middle initial, not that he as an individual has no worth.

Because of the date: August 24, 1961, it seems likely that this verse was read at the end of the Education Council as a thank you to Kenneth for a course that he gave during those teachers' meetings. The versifier added this note: "With frustration and gratitude, L.H."

12
To KR

With Mr. Kenneth (Nothing) Rose
Any word or number goes
Farther than you'd think it would.
He knows two languages are good—
The one of math, the other word;
Knows what's absurd and also surd.
He knows his plus and minus signs,
Toward balances he most inclines;
Puts commas in or cuts them out;
Knows pretty nearly all about
Tradition and experiment,
Moonwatch math, homemade cement,
The fine abstract, the gross concrete,
Degrees continuous and discrete,
Composing hymns and reading Greek,
The standard product and the freak,
Quanta, cliques, and other sets,
The probable outcome of bets,
Figures Roman, Arabic,
Calculus, arithmetic
Little children and adults,
Silly problems, sad results,
Euclid's axioms, Newton's laws,
And something of the Final Cause.

Idealist and pragmatist,
There is not much that he has missed—
Deducing this, inducing that,
Aristocrat and democrat.

August 24, 1961

This verse was written for Jane and Stanley Ebert's 25th wedding anniversary. It is a tribute to them especially for their part in organizing and conducting a trip to France for interested students from the Academy. Besides sight-seeing, the trip included a stay in the homes of French families that spoke little or no English. It was a chance for immersion in a foreign language that was unequaled by classroom experience. And it was, as Lyris says, a great success.

On a copy of the poem sent to the Eberts after the party Lyris appended this note:

> *This isn't exactly the version you heard. I found that in my hurried copying of my scribbled notes I had left out a line. And some of the lines were so bad I just had to fix them up a little.*
>
> *With haste but with affection,*
>
> Lyris

13

For Stan and Jane—October 8, 1960

A quarter century's gone by
Plus three days more—how time does fly—
Since our friends Stan and Jane joined forces,
A fact this company endorses
Most heartily. You ask us why?
We're glad to give you our reply:
We say that Stan has *savoir faire*
And so has Jane; in fact this pair
Is quite *au fait*, never *de trop*,
Good sports, and always apropos.
Our manly Stanley (in the main)
And our dame Jane are plainly sane
Except when trips to France are planned
For undergrads. Now we demand
To know their secret of success.
They didn't rate a gruesome mess,
But how could such a trip abroad
That participants and parents laud
Work out so well? They gave the chance
To New Church students to enhance
Their international point of view
By living as the French folk do.
It worked, and we are proud it did,
That students did what they were bid,
For students are prone to label "fraud"
Whatever fails. We're glad to applaud
This venturesome couple with heart and head.
We're pleased that Stan and Jane have said
They're proud of New Church girls and boys—
Their manners, charity, and poise.
We love them both; so here's a toast
For Stan and Jane—They are the most.

Lyris wrote this for Mary Lou Williamson's October birthday in 1967. At that time "Miss Mary Lou" was still teaching in the kindergarten where she had been for many happy years. This *is* a happy poem. It recalls the delights of childhood memories in the many allusions to Fairy Tales and Nursery Rhymes, especially in the long third stanza.

14

Mary Lou and Her Little Lambs

Mary Lou has some little lambs
Into whose heads and hearts she crams
(Or maybe she figures and fits with care
All these things, both homely and fair):

Shadows and sunshine, flowers and birds,
Puzzles, pictures, numbers and words,
Books and blocks, dance and song,
Two by two, by threes or a throng;
Jumping for joy, quiet gladness,
Listening long, sounds of sadness:

One little—two little—thises and thats:
Prince and frog, Hamelin rats,
All the king's horses, sacks and kittens,
Petticoats, pinafores, socks and mittens,
Queen-looking, Cheshire, Whittington cats,
Jack and Jill, compatible Sprats,
Pantalettes, Pirouettes, Pantaloons,
Cupboards, cabbages, runcible spoons,
Marmalade, honey from bees in a tree,
Milk and porridge, camomile tea,
Gammon and spinach, jumbles and jam,
Dunmow bacon, flitch, or ham,
Blackbird pies and pockets of rye,
Cockles, puddings, and simple pie,
Curds and whey and hot cross buns,
Strawberries, cream, and Sally Lunns,
Flapjacks, gingerbread, hot corn pone,
White bread and butter, cheese alone;

Farmer, miller, soldier, sailor
(From the dell or from Dee), and Gloucester tailor,
Sticks and stones and wishing bone,
Dwarves and elves, princess and crone.

Miss Mary Lou lives under a hill,
And many are happy she lives there still.

October 7, 1967

For Mama was written for an occasion—the anniversary of the marriage of the Hubert Hyatts. But it is by no means what we would call "light verse." As her father was no longer living on earth, Lyris's poem has a serious tone, but it is not sad. It expresses the fervent hope of many widows to be reunited with their husbands in the life after death with the promise of true and eternal marriage in heaven.

15

For Mama

An anniversary—
But what are years?
The same old nursery
Of hopes and fears.

This needful time and space
Must serve our turn.
Yet we, in human case,
Deem all laws stern.

But all goes as it should:
The Lord works still for good;
And she will meet again
Her husband—of all men
The only one she loved. What thrill!
We know it's true. She wills. She will.

February 11, 1966

Another serious poem was written on the occasion of the death of Alice Henderson Glenn, October 9, 1964. Lyris gave the poem to Bruce Glenn and the children as an expression of her understanding and sympathy.

In November of the same year she revised the sonnet somewhat and gave it the title **The Readiness Is All** from Hamlet V ii and sent it to the Poetry Society of America.

Then in the summer of 1965 while taking a course at Bread Loaf in "The Craft of Poetry," Lyris worked on the poem again and retitled it **No Hecuba.** It is the 1965 version that is printed here.

The following are some portions of a note directed to Mr. Nims about the poem.

> *The comment in class about the* Iliad *did not seem ridiculous to me. It is true, as you guessed, that I did not think of the* Iliad *when I wrote the sonnet but my title is a direct reference to the Trojan story, and it must have been what Shakespeare was thinking of. Hecuba was nothing to the bereaved husband for whom I wrote my sonnet, and yet he was (and is) much interested in feelings about someone who does not touch us personally—in the particular that is not particular to* us: *in* art.
>
> *I think that most poems should not be derivative, and should not demand special knowledge, but this one, with its eight or so allusions to Shakespeare (mostly* Hamlet*) is written for a special audience of one. He knows* Hamlet *well, and he is especially fond of Sonnet 116. He has given a good lecture on art, based on "What's Hecuba to him—or he to Hecuba."*
>
> *This is the only "poem" I ever wrote while I was feeling emotional. I wrote it the morning after Alice died. I wanted to do something for Bruce to let him know I was aware and cared. Bruce writes pretty good sonnets. This was my answer. I have revised the first try twice—once for sense, and once to make it more universal. . . .*
>
> *I wonder how many readers will continue the last line from Horatio (Hamlet I, i) and echo quietly: "and do in part believe it."*

16

No Hecuba

(for a Shakespearean friend on the death of his young wife)

'Why seems it so particular with thee?'
It always does. It is. We know not 'seems.'
And when it comes to her, to you, to me,
We do not look at first for abstract themes.
The universal is particular.
The finite hearts involved are limited.
It's not the milky way but one fixed star
That is our cynosure. The tears we shed
Are, for a while, for one—then for the few
Touched to the quick. We swear there is no art
To make us fully ready for our cue
To take the stage tonight and play our part.

How can one suit his action to this word?
But somehow you go on—or so I've heard.

Revised July 5, 1965

Part III
Christmas Poems

Beginning with a poem called "Christmas" written in 1961 and up until 1976, Lyris wrote more than a dozen Christmas poems which she sent out as her Advent greeting to her friends. These poems contain allusions and references to the Old and New Testaments and the Heavenly Doctrines. They are truly New Church Christmas cards.

Five of them have been selected for this book. Two: "Christmas Tidings" and "All We Like Sheep" were previously printed in the *Theta Alpha Journal*.

17

Christmas Tidings

Another year has darkened down
but once again the tide is turning
toward the light.

The promise that we need not drown
renewed for us, the dear star burning
far but bright,

we know the dark for what it is,

Let's put it by
and thank the Lord that we are His.

O magnify
with love the Dayspring from on high.

1964

18

The End Is Peace

It's strange: He is called the Prince of Peace,
Yet He came to bring not peace but a sword.
But truth is strange. He makes wars cease
For all who subserve His will. The Lord
Discharges His soldiers, gives full release
When they've won that war they once abhorred.

Psalm 37:37, *Life* 95

1965

19

Given—This Day

We cannot tell the stars
or number the sands of the shore
but we can look to the East
and answer the knock at our door.

We can watch for and follow one star,
walk on in the narrow way,
fed by the heavenly bread
given to us each day

and come in time to know the worth
of the Word this day come down to earth.

1966

20

All We Like Sheep...

We do not like our likenesses to sheep.
And yet we wear their clothes, are often lost,
ignore the sheepfold door and the Shepherd's voice.

That holy night the shepherds did not sleep.
The Shepherd sacrificed Himself—the cost
of life for all His flock. His careful choice

we carelessly forget. Recall: the Lord foretold
that other sheep will hear, that there shall be one fold.

1967

21

In such an hour...*

The simple shepherds watched their flock by night.
The wise men, waiting, must have watched as well.
In such an hour as they thought not, He came.

Those shepherds in simplicity saw light,
took fright, but took the tidings too, could tell
what they should do, and knew the Lord by name.

Those wise men in their wisdom knew at sight
the meaning of the star. They came and fell
upon their knees, gave gifts, and felt no shame.

As we bide with the flock in our field and scan our skies,
may we come to be wisely simple or simply wise.

1970

*Matt. 24:44, 25:13

Part IV
Bread Loaf

Lyris had a love affair with Bread Loaf, or to be more specific, The Bread Loaf School of English of Middlebury College in Vermont. She attended the mountain campus in the summer of 1955 and then from 1957-1961 on, earning an MA in English at the end of that last summer session. After her graduation Lyris returned to Bread Loaf several times as an auditor and visitor, notably in 1965 when she took a course with John Frederick Nims in "The Craft of Poetry."

She spoke often to her colleagues in the ANC English Department about the benefits of the courses and life at Bread Loaf and influenced several of them to attend. Two, Janna King Odhner and Vera Powell Glenn, are fellow graduates of the Bread Loaf School of English because of her conviction of its excellence.

In August 1976 Lyris wrote this endorsement. It speaks in her own voice of the delights, both intellectual and natural, which she found at Bread Loaf and explains why she returned there so often to refresh her spirit.

Every Teacher Should Have It So Good

If you are an *English teacher*—old or young, fresh or tired, confident or intimidated—at the Bread Loaf School of English (Middlebury College's graduate summer school in English) you can

earn your Master's degree—or, if you already have one, another

enjoy birds, wildflowers, meadows, brooks, woods, and mountains

regain a (your?) student's point of view

take one or two courses that you need—either for your job or for yourself

learn to be a better teacher without taking another methods course

see Robert Frost's country—and the cabin where he lived and wrote

sharpen your mind and refresh your spirit

be taught by a distinguished faculty of scholar-teachers from different universities

be taken to Emily Dickinson's "Lands away" without continual packing and unpacking

swim, hike, jog, walk, or stroll; play tennis, volleyball, softball, or croquet

hear outstanding visiting lecturers

choose from some two dozen courses the one or two that seem best to fill your needs

be cooler than at almost any American university

be known by your teachers as an individual—by name

be stimulated by sharing ideas with your peers

benefit from the rigor of the courses and the informality of the Bread Loaf life

restore your rightful sense of your usefulness and dignity

take part in dramatic productions—or simply attend them

strengthen the courage of your convictions—or modify them

confirm, modify, or reverse your approaches to teaching "English"

see films—mostly classics of various kinds

enjoy going to school without having to prepare the classes, grade the papers, or compose the exams; walk out from an exam and let someone else deal with what you have done

realize that a change is often as good as a rest

exercise your freedom by by-passing any number of all these Bread Loaf offerings.

August 1976

The Crumb is the daily newssheet of the Bread Loaf School of English. Excerpts from the July 27, 1955 issue carry some interesting items as well as the first poem Lyris had printed in *The Crumb*. It has no title, simply called "Contribution," and no author's name given.

A few notes may make some things clearer:

The Bread Loaf Inn, once a coach stop on the Middlebury pass through the Green Mountains, is used as the administration building, dining hall, and main dormitory of the campus. Lyris had a room there on the 3rd floor for many summers. The fire in the lobby was not a disaster, but a comfort. On cold, drizzly mountain days the wood fires in the lobby and the blue parlor were very welcome even in summer.

The Inn is surrounded on three sides by a wide, vine-hung porch with old-fashioned wooden rockers and benches. After dinner students would often take their coffee there.

The Barn was used not for hay or animals, but as a social center. Coffee in the Barn during a break in morning classes was a necessity (for those who missed breakfast) and a pleasure for all who liked intellectual exchange with classmates and teachers.

Part of the Bread Loaf summer is the theatre. The Theatre Arts course is strenuous for players and crew, with two major productions in six weeks. Lyris was in that course in the summer of 1955. It probably only *seemed* like 13 dress rehearsals.

"A's and double-checks" refer to the grades or marks on papers, as do "the D's and X." The last are two marks which Lyris never saw.

THE CRUMB

Volume 36, No. 21 Bread Loaf, Vermont July 27, 1955

Radax Malorum Est Cupiditas

To allow for clearance, the Middlebury banks set the following date lines for cashing checks:

West of the Mississippi—July 28 (tomorrow)
Southern States—July 30
New York, New Jersey, New England—August 5

Teaching Position

Mrs. Lettie Lee Craig, Ass't. to the Director
Cherry Lawn School
Darien, Connecticut

Mrs. Craig is looking for a single man with some experience (in teaching English), but not too old to enjoy dormitory duty with adolescents. The teacher would be expected to take on the student publications work and perhaps teach one class in social studies. Cherry Lawn is a co-educational school of excellent rating. It is a college-preparatory boarding school forty miles from the Big City. No salary scale has been given, but it is probably quite fine.

Mr. Frost Tomorrow Night

After Mr. Frost speaks on Puritanism in the Barn tomorrow night, he will be willing to answer any questions on poetry that Bread Loafers may have. Please submit your questions to Mr. Cook before then.

From the Bookstore

The Bookstore is pleased to announce that it will hold open house daily from 1:45 to 2 P.M.

A copy of Cubeta, *Modern Drama for Analysis,* was inadvertently sent to the bookstore by our downtown competitor. Since the high standards of our store do not allow us to peddle such truck, will the purchaser of the thing please remove it from the bookstore as soon as possible.

A Contribution

There's a fire in the lobby,
And my ironing didn't scorch.
There is coffee in the barn,
There'll be coffee on the porch.
There's mail in most the boxes,
There is tennis on the courts.
There's basking in the sunshine
With repartee—of sorts.

There are thirteen dress rehearsals,
There are A's and double-checks.
There's a splendid milky way—
Forget the D's and X.
It ought to keep me happy,
But the summer's creeping on;
I love the life at Bread Loaf,
But the loaf's half gone.

Under no circumstances will the editor reveal the author of this poem.

In the summer of 1958 Lyris took a writing course with the poet William Meredith, which changed her from a writer of occasional verse and poems for students to a serious poet. She calls **Bright and Dark** written July 1958 her first real poem (see no. 31, Part V).

Again in 1959 at Bread Loaf Lyris had a course, English 17—Elements of Writing, with Mr. Meredith, who was apparently an inspiring teacher. His comments helped to guide Lyris through numerous revisions to a surer voice and stronger form in her poems. The following notes between teacher and student, the crossings-out and changes in wording and structure show how a poem is made.

Lyris attached this note to the poem **Love-light** when she first handed it to the teacher.

Hyatt 17 *Love-light*

This is a try at following your advice not to bother too much about form and was probably written more quickly than almost anything I have finished. What you said in class about the importance of the first and last words in a line has helped. The point is sensible of course, but I had never been conscious of it before.

Is the ambiguity of the last line bad? I think I am content to have it understood almost any way so long as the "tease" is taken to mean a possible taking-seriously.

I don't like line 9 very well, and don't like the fact that there are so many ease *rhymes.*

The revisions, in pencil, were begun after she received the following comments from the teacher.

> *"Love-light" is as unobtrusive, for most of its length, as you can hope to make couplets, I guess. The ease-rhymes are obtrusive because they are 4, and because, I agree, line 9, (and line 8 as well), is not quite natural. "not peak/uneasy" is weak, especially after "why don't they . . ." Chaff and laugh are a tired old rhyme, but the thing that I object to more than that is the unnaturalness of chaff in any modern usage: it gives the poem an arch tone, I feel.*
>
> WM

24

Love-light (a)

If I in love lack levity and ease,

Lose all proportion, look as sad as these

Poor couples seem, who ~~stroll and~~ saunter smile and sit

Quite unengaged with anyone, I'll quit,

Be rational, be sane. Why don't they ~~chaff~~ laugh

At silly consequential things ~~and laugh~~

Out loud so I must almost envy; speak,

Commit themselves with more than eyes, ~~not peak~~

~~Uneasy, clutched by such unspeakable disease~~

~~Or dreariness and~~ kill themselves to please?

Chaffling

~~At last~~ I love: I'm heavy, ill at ease,

Self-conscious and could die. Why must you tease

Me? Seriously, I am contrite.

Make my yoke easy, your burden light.

July 28, 1959

With her second version Lyris attached this brief note:

I doubt that this yet goes as well as it could, but at least it feels heaps better, thanks.

Love-light (b)

If I in love lack levity and ease,
Lose all proportion, look as sad as those
Poor couples do, who saunter by, ~~and~~ smile
And sit quite unengaged with anyone,
I'll quit, be rational again. O why —
I very nearly ask —why don't you laugh
Out loud at silly consequential things
To make me almost envy you, commit
Yourselves with more than eyes and ~~[illegible] hands?~~ helpless hands?
Love's surely not unspeakable entirely;
~~Live~~ Talk a bit, ~~don't~~ do not kill yourselves to please.

Tonight at last I am in love ~~and will~~
And I'll At ease, so heavy that ~~I am silent~~ I am silent!
~~And~~ I long to follow my too smug advice.
~~But~~ No, please don't tease me ~~now~~ — take me ~~seriously~~
Seriously For once. / ~~No,~~ Oh I was right I guess: / stay gay, light;
Make my ~~yoke~~ role easy, keep your burden ~~light~~ blithe ~~a~~ for while.

July 20, 1959

See what happens in the poem between versions 2 and 3. Although version 2 "feels better" as Lyris says, the further revisions make version 3 the best.

Love-light (c)

If I in love lack levity and ease,
Lose all proportion, look as sad as those
Poor couples do, who saunter by, smile,
And sit quite unengaged with anyone
Except themselves, I'll quit, be rational
Again.

    Oh why—
I very nearly ask—why don't you laugh
Out loud at silly consequential things
To make me almost envy you, commit
Yourselves with more than eyes and helpless hands?
Love's surely not unspeakable entirely.
Talk out a bit; don't kill yourselves to please.

Tonight at last it seems I am in love
And ill at ease, so heavy I am silent!
I long to follow my too smug advice.

No, please don't tease; take me seriously
For once.

    Oh I was right before I guess: be blithe,
Make my role easy, keep your burden light for a while.

July 28, 1959

Mr. Meredith's classes included many aspiring poets, and it is probably there that Lyris met Jonathan Aldrich. She wrote the little poem (across the page) **You Are** for him.

Later in the summer Jonathan wrote a poem about Lyris called "Croquet Lover at the Dinner Table." (While at Bread Loaf Lyris was an avid player of croquet on the lawn behind the Inn.)

Over the years Lyris and Jonathan corresponded from time to time encouraging each other to keep writing. In 1977 Jonathan wrote to tell Lyris he was having a book of poetry published, and Lyris wrote to the publisher the following letter.

The University of Missouri Press
107 Swallow Hall
Columbia, Missouri 65201

Gentlemen:

I understand that in March you are publishing a volume of poetry by Jonathan Aldrich entitled Croquet Lover at the Dinner Table. I relished the title poem when I read it some eighteen years ago and look forward to seeing more poems by Mr. Aldrich. I used to tell him he should publish and am glad he and you have gotten together.

Please send me one copy as soon as possible. My check for $6.25 is enclosed.

Yours sincerely,

Lyris Hyatt

How delicately she implies her friendship with the author yet refrains from mentioning that she was the subject of the title poem.

25

You Are.*

Young—old;—ageless;
Quick—still—timeless;
Wild thyme blowing
Rageless. Sage.

1958

**In reply to a young friend who earnestly asked, "What am I?"*

26

Croquet Lover at the Dinner Table

She passes muffins, orders the most remote
and sudden relishes, comments on
the one particular poem you meant to keep
entirely undiscussed, or interrupts
your train of silence with a stab
of curiosity on what you plan
to do next year if love or money won't
come through, as if it were a game
to find you out: to slam you out of court,
to rout the field, dislodge the set-up shot,
provoke your aim, suggest a change of rules
until you feel immeasurably behind
because her eyes are never wicketed,
dead on nobody and poison to the last.

(written by Jonathan Aldrich 1958)

The Falls was written in 1959 at Bread Loaf. The physical backdrop is a most beautiful waterfall, with the improbable name of Texas Falls, on a clear mountain stream about ten miles from the campus.

In a winter letter to Jonathan who was not at Bread Loaf in 1959 Lyris described the summer and the experience which led to the writing of this poem.

Bryn Athyn
February 12, 1960
9:30 p.m.

Dear Jonathan,

The summer had lots of highlights. I can hardly believe that I had never seen Texas Falls before but I hadn't. Having Morna's car helped. Also Mike Pulman's obvious horror that I hadn't been. So a bunch of us went. A couple of times we took lunch. Later we found that Mr. Meredith had never been either and took him after I had written a long poem about the falls for his course. (Time to go. More later sometime.)

2/14. I didn't think that my Falls poem was so bad when I finished it, but now I don't like it very much although I don't seem to be able to revise it. Just to encourage you to send me some of yours I'll enclose it with this letter, with the high-schoolish reminder that the "you" isn't really anyone. I don't really know what Mr. Meredith thought of it. He was impressed in a way but didn't think I had really pictured what the place was like. I was pleased that he thought the falls themselves were really beautiful. The part about the Milton is fairly factual. Rick Asals and I were in the course and agreed that we had too much studying to do to go to the falls, but then about six of us made a pact that we would really study before we went swimming. We dispersed ourselves all over the rocks—Mary Dunham (who wrote delightful short stories for the advanced course)—looked like a pixy sitting cross-legged on the flat rock surrounded by water and typing away seemingly oblivious of everything. Rick and I were reading Comus *out loud but didn't disturb anyone because of the sound of the water. . . .*

But the epigraph indicates that more is going on in the poem than the simple recording of an experience. The last lines tie in with the child in the quotation from the Word and suggest a kind of rebirth of the spirit, a recapturing of the innocence of the Garden of Eden in the perfection of natural creation.

27

The Falls

Behold, this child is set for the fall and rising again of many in Israel; and for a sign which shall be spoken against; (Yea, a sword shall pierce through thy own soul also.) that the thoughts of many hearts may be revealed.

1

I'd heard about the lovely falls of course;
We all had. Lots of you would go there; still
I hadn't gone: they sounded much too good
For truth and not a place where I could do
The work I thought I had to do to school
Myself. I might have gone if I had had
My own car, or certain friends had asked me, but....

2

This year I have a car, one lent to me
By her who is the other half of what
I should be, warm yet mathematic hearted,
With mind enough for two; she's in Aegean
Islands, writes of Aeschylus, feels all too well
What I need to read from her, and mentions
Not a word about the car she owns
Or the double set of keys she gave to me
To fill the need that she herself knows too.

3

It was to be a sober trip, I said:
We'd take our books and work, not be decoyed
By bird or water song to leave the rocks
Until we'd done our stint of Milton.
But forty minutes later, lengthening shades
Made all of them agree, with a word or two,
That they were ready for their swim. They set
Out for the pool, leaping down from rock
To bank and back, with kindly jeers as usual
At my silly boast that first I'd finish off
Book Nine. They disappeared beyond the trees.

Turning another page, I looked downstream
Toward where they'd gone and saw you
Standing gay and insolent high on a boulder,
Waving a dare to me to follow.

I stood up,
And though you now were out of sight, put down my book.

4

You had gone so easily (from practice
Now I know) that I perversely chose
A path less difficult though longer. Never sure
Of foot, I could not make the springs you others
Did, but plodded through the woods alone,

Slipping in slime, bruising the bones of my foot
On the root of an old spruce, nearly blind from
Ducking under scratchy branches, sticky-handed
From grabbing a resinous log when I lost my balance.

And there, below, it was:
the falls a downward fountain—
Gush filling the curiously scoured hollow
Worn in the whale-humped elephant hide
Of gray-green, wood-grained stone;
Zircon emerald water marbled through
With tempered light; deep and surely cold.

Shivering, I listened for your voices:
Nothing but the surfy roar and subtle chill.

I knew one shouldn't swim alone, but too impatient
Now to wait to take a plunge, I partly slid,
Half fell to the gravel beach, and waded in.

5

At last.
In—and under water unstrangely warming
After what you'd guess would be a shock—
Free, in a partly emptied Easter egg
Shell cracked open to blue sky and all the gold

Of sun framed in leaves and needles, focused

As if for me alone. And sound!—such noise
Of living waters pouring down with Wagner crash
Pounding.
                But clean and quiet too as oboe
Shepherd's pipe or Isolde's trusting air;
And underneath, a resonant organ bass
Resounding from arched walls abraded through all times
To beauty, almost, nearly, perfect.

Colder now, I listened again for your voices,
Heard them echo far below, and waiting,
Hardly swam, but, body borne along
In current generated by the falls,
Breathlessly I came upon a barely submerged
Rock, and clung, breast to stone,
More cold and lonely, naturally, than when I read
And rested on the sunburnt rocks above.

6

And then you came.
                Astonishing, around the hugest boulder,
Slipping over the saddle of stone smoothly into the pool,
Laughing, as I was suddenly, at the joke that had no point or sting.

7

So this is what it is, has always been,
Through all that dreadful time of time and space.
I never even dreamed that, absent-minded, I
(Only for moments unself-centered)—that you
And I were present here, together, in what is really central:
This homely spacious house, this absolutely perfect haven
That I've hoped for, doubting all the while that it
Existed.
                Mist in eyes, confounded with
This loveliness, I'm joyed not even overly
To realize I can accept these gifts
Of mercy as the child I never was till now.

July 1959

Lyris wrote again to Jonathan in April 1960:

Even before your letter came (early in March?) I had read over the falls poem and begun cutting fairly drastically. It helped, but not enough. That it helped you to get writing again is use enough for it—at least for now. Your letter was an impetus toward further effort of some kind. I got about eight passable but pedestrian lines for Robert Frost's 86th birthday.

The month before she had sent the poem to Robert Frost along with the following letter:

Bryn Athyn, Pennsylvania
March 6, 1960

Mr. Robert Frost
Ripton, Vermont

Dear Mr. Frost,

Although they don't do what I wanted them to do, here are a few lines to wish you a happy birthday. You have given me a lot of exercise and fun, both at Bread Loaf and here alone with your poems, and somehow I have caught the disease of trying to put words together. Thank you very much.

Yours sincerely,

Lyris

(There is no indication that she ever received a reply.)

For many years Robert Frost lived on a small farm in Ripton, Vermont, a few miles down the road from Bread Loaf. Frost was a frequent visitor and lecturer on the campus. (See *The Crumb*, July 27, 1955, no. 23.) Lyris was fortunate to be on campus during the time when the poet was often there. In the Barn after his lectures and readings there was a chance to get acquainted with him on an informal basis.

Some of Lyris's poems reflect the Frostian turn of phrase, and this birthday poem has echoes of several of his poems. It was published in *The Crumb* on July 12, 1960. It was never published anywhere else, although Lyris sent it to several magazines for consideration.

28

For Mr. Frost

I guess for most his four score years and six
He's had his fun, has known the proper fix
We're in, has owned and honored holy fears,
The cost of feeling—acting, being—free;
Seen fairly clear that freedom disappears
When rudely we insist security
Shall be provided. Only choice abides.
We can't evade the risks that it provides.

March 26, 1960

In Mr. Nims's course "The Craft of Poetry," which Lyris took at Bread Loaf in the summer of 1965, the following exercise was set:

Write a sonnet in which the lines end with the words
bread,
loaf,
red,
oaf,
summer,
school,
dumber,
pool,
much,
work,
such,
quirk,
free,
degree.

Here on the next page is Lyris's result with a catchy title.

Grades were a source of much discussion and some discontent at Bread Loaf. It was difficult for English teachers to submit to criticism and marking as if they were students. Some felt there should be no grades, and others that the grades should only be A's and B's. Lyris's observations were apt, and by this time, as a graduate, she could afford to be detached.

Lyris labeled this poem:

Sonnet exercise
Middleweight verse
Structure: 12 #2 (ex post facto)

29

Superior Student Regards Superior Students Regarding Superior Professors

Ready to butter up, they ask for bread.
They think they do—but don't see half a loaf
As more than just a slice. How they see red
And sulk! They'd like: to stone the pedant oaf,
To stab, to have his guts. But it is summer
And much too hot, so they resolve to school
Themselves to play it cool. The glib get dumber;
The bashful find a word or two and pool
Their tearful indignation. It's too much!
He underrates the really brilliant work
That some of them have done: research, as such
—and published (but for an editorial quirk).

It's good, I guess, that none of us is free
From apple-polishing . . . to *some* degree.

July 25, 1965

Nothing of Consequence was first written in the end of July 1965. A heading on one copy of the poem calls it "An *exercise* in Poetry." Probably it was written for Mr. Nims's course and then revised later.

It does have a Bread Loaf setting and draws on a then common practice at the school—the taking of evening walks after dinner. The traditional stroll was along the road, past Tamarack Cottage, up the gentle slope and down into the dip where a culvert carried a little stream under the road and the white-throated sparrows whistled sweetly in the evergreens. Usually, then, the pedestrians turned and headed back, if they had gotten so far. In the poem the couple comes back a different way, but even breaking the pattern of the walk doesn't seem to have gotten them anywhere. "*The non-discussibility of love,*" the last line reads.

This inability to communicate inner feelings, especially to talk of love, echoes the idea expressed earlier in **Love-light** (see no. 24c).

> "Love's surely not unspeakable entirely.
> Talk out a bit.
>
> Tonight at last it seems I am in love,
> And ill at ease, so heavy I am silent."

A poet finds it particularly frustrating not to be able to use words to express the mind and heart because words are the stuff of the writer's life.

While this idea of the two poems is similar, the technique of each is very different. **Nothing of Consequence** arises directly from experience with specific images to carry immediacy. The lines have an easy swing, like walking (in iambic pentameter, the meter that Frost once called natural to English poetry).

The last line holds the realization as it concludes and includes the whole poem.

30

Nothing of Consequence

Come take a walk, he said, and off they went.
They strode at first, but then slowed down so much
That when they'd reached the crest by Tamarack,
Their usual turning point, it seemed too late
To keep on being sensible about
and of—the place and time.
        Let papers wait;
That poem could rework itself for all
She cared; and that old frigate book could stay
Unsailed for one more day.
        The road ahead,
As well as that behind, led down, then up.
The easy going down felt good, of course.
They talked about it some, in metaphor—
The ins and outs, the highs and lows, the middle
Ground. Still, there really wasn't much to add
To what they hadn't said before, so often.
His reticence and her timidity
That made her gossip helplessly along
Were hopeless incompatibilities.

In time they doubled back along the trail
Beyond the old deserted house and past
The burial ground. When they got back to the Inn
Long after dark, the student lamps burned bright.

The ups and downs, she thought—the craziness,
The doublesidedness of everything,
Inconsequentialities—or worse:
The non-discussibility of love.

July 31, 1965

Part V
Poems: Bright and Dark

This may have been Lyris's first rejection slip. It is certainly an informal one and shows that even a well-known poet and user of words like John Ciardi can slip up, using "life" for like.

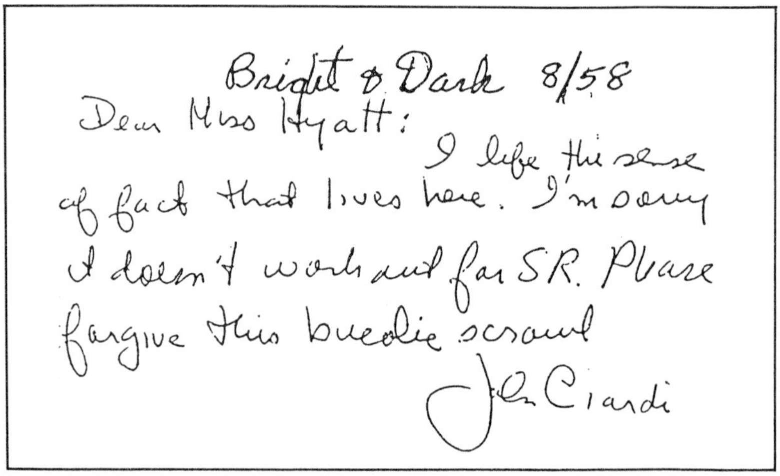
Bright & Dark 8/58
Dear Miss Hyatt:
I life the sense of fact that lives here. I'm sorry it doesn't work out for S.R. Please forgive this bucolic scrawl
John Ciardi

It was after her stimulating summer course at Bread Loaf in 1958 that Lyris began to write seriously and to think of herself as a poet (though only a modest one). She sent out her best poems to a variety of magazines, keeping careful note in a special spiral notebook of the date sent, and the date rejected. Over the years she accumulated a lot of rejection slips from *The New Yorker, Saturday Review, Ladies Home Journal, Poetry, Saturday Evening Post, Atlantic Monthly, Hudson Review, English Journal*, and others. Although these rejections must have hurt, she kept them, with her wry sense of humor comparing them for the variety and courtesy (or lack of it) of ways they said "No." Some even added comments of which she kept track.

> Atlantic: *You write with a facility which has held our attention.*
>
> Sat. Eve. Post: ***Mean Teacher*** *came very close. Try us again!*
>
> American Weave: *Had we the space, I think we would have kept* **The Falls.** *I don't know where I might suggest that you send a poem of this length, but I do hope that you find a home for it.*
>
> Sixties: *I like* **Bright and Dark** *the best of these,* though they do seem a little too talkative.*

*On March 20, 1961 Lyris sent to *Sixties*, among other poems: **Bright and Dark, Emendation, Verbose,** and **Two Aunts and the Two- year-old**. All were rejected.

The writing of **Bright and Dark** began a new phase in Lyris's poetic development. She calls it her first poem. Not that she hadn't written poems before, but that this was her first serious poem, or perhaps, the first poem she took seriously.

The title seems very significant. For from that time on most of the poems express this duality, a dichotomy of feeling: joy and sadness, faith and doubt, confidence and self-effacement, trust in future fulfillment and longing. The elements of bright and dark are, of course, common to all human life. I like the balance that Lyris gets between them, rather than having one poem all shade and another sunlight.

31

Bright and Dark

The first time he remembered I took cream
In coffee—long ago—I smiled inside
And hugged the thought I had a pigeonhole
At least. But that was all. Anyway
I learned quite soon to take my coffee black.

I made a yellow dress with sash and frills
And hardly trembled when his friend one May
Came home with me and played his saxophone
And laughed at what I said my brother said
In school. He moved that June. I put on weight
And found I looked more slim and old in sheaths.

And now that I am old and thin I don't
Know what to drink or wear. With soft and hard
And bright and dark it's easy now to alternate
Between the two. When will you look at me
And see I am not always hard and fast
And know I am not really hard—or easy.

(My first poem July 1958)

Published in *The Bread Loaf Poets*, July 1958

Then in December 1959 Lyris received instead of a rejection, a letter from Llewellyn Jones, literary editor of *The Humanist* saying that three of her poems had been accepted! Typically straightforward she wrote back, in part:

Dear Mr. Jones:

Thank you for your interest in my poems. Although I think that I am basically opposed to the philosophy represented by The Humanist, *you are welcome to print "To Live at Home," "Snares of Spring," and "Set for Snow." Not getting paid for them doesn't bother me, but I would appreciate receiving a copy of the issue in which they appear. If you can't manage to send me a copy free, I am willing to pay for it.*

It is somewhat ironic that yours is the first acceptance I have received. It was the listing of John Holmes (in a writers' magazine) as poetry editor that gave me the impetus to send in some of my stuff. The magazine staff would consider me subversive to its movement because I believe that the Old and New Testaments are divine revelation and authority and can be rightly understood by rational people through the explanation of their internal meaning as revealed in the theological works of Emanuel Swedenborg. I believe that the Greek myths originally expressed the same truths. . . .

As for the biographical sketch, I'll leave that to you to do as you like. The facts are these: Lyris Hyatt wrote no verse until 1958 and has published none (except for a couple of pieces in a small, mimeographed church magazine and a mimeographed selection of student work). She is a graduate of The Academy of the New Church College and has attended the Bread Loaf School of English for four summers. She teaches in the Girls School of The Academy of the New Church, Bryn Athyn, Pa.

Thanks again for the delightful shock of your letter.

Although it looked as if she was on the way, Mr. Jones died; two of the poems were lost in the shuffle, and it was the new editor, Judson Jerome, who almost two years later printed **To Live at Home** in *The Humanist* May-June 1961.

Except for the year at Columbia working on her master's degree in education and the summers spent at Bread Loaf, Lyris lived in her childhood home on Alnwick Road all her life. It would have been natural for her to leave the Hubert Hyatt house for a new home at the time of her marriage, but Lyris never did marry and never moved. Making the adjustments to living as an adult in the place and with the parents that one has known as a child isn't easy. Is this what Lyris means by learning "to live at home/With glasses on"?

Lyris was myopic, and she wore lenses of some kind most of her life to correct this visual problem. She recounted often the joy of getting her first pair of glasses when she could at last see the leaves on the trees.

Although blurring the edges of things often makes them softer and prettier, Lyris liked to see things clearly. This poem is about seeing. Here she uses the concrete images of physical sight to show the individual's need for defined relationships—for seeing both the forest and the trees.

32

To Live at Home

Distance can make the heart grow far too fond,
Too vague or vaporish, too credulous
That time and space will erase edginess
    For good and all:

    Home is a haze,
    friends' faces shade
    to softness, words
    heard in memory
    fade and glow,
    re-understood
    in mists of love's
    myopia.

I'll have to learn in time to live at home
With glasses on, disowning those enchantments
That distance only lends but cannot give.

July 1958

First published in *The Humanist*, Nos. 5 & 6, 1961

The path between writers and publishers probably never runs smoothly, but none could be rougher than that between Lyris and *Poetry Digest.*

In January 1960, her poem **Bookshelf Bibelots** was accepted by the magazine for publication. Excited at the prospect of seeing her poem in print Lyris took out a subscription for a year, and received one issue. No further issues were forthcoming and no word about her poem either.

The letter on the facing page is printed in full because it so neatly encapsulates the whole experience.

33

April 25, 1961

Mr. John De Stefano, Editor
Poetry Digest
P.O. Box 177
Milldale, Conn.

Dear Mr. Stefano:

Recently I was wondering whether I would ever see more than the one number of your magazine which I received last spring. It was with some surprise, therefore, that this morning I received two copies for April 1961. I am glad to see that you are back in business again.

However, I am now astonished to find my "Bookshelf Bibelots" included. And I am distressed to find that the next-to-last word in line 6 has been changed from these to them—which makes comparative nonsense. I think it would be only fair to note this correction in your next issue and shall be grateful if you are courteous enough to do so.

My astonishment may be a surprise to you if you did not read a number of communications I sent you last summer and fall. My August 18th letter suggested that you return my poem. My September 16th letter enclose a stamped envelope for the return of the manuscript. My postcard of October 5th urged you to return the manuscript or to send me a line stating definitely what had happened to it. I also asked, if it had been mislaid, that you destroy it if it ever turned up.

My letter of October 15th (of which I hold a sealed copy mailed to myself and postmarked) reviewed my previous requests and said in part: "I now consider that you have forfeited any right to my poem 'Bookshelf Bibelots' and that I may now offer it for publication elsewhere without restriction. If your understanding is in any way in disagreement with mine, I shall expect to hear from you within five days."

Since you never said anything about the fate of my poem, I felt free to offer it to another publication, which I did. It was published last month. It is a little embarrassing to me, but more embarrassing for you since you have published a poem to which you had no right.*

Yours truly,
Lyris Hyatt

*Ed. note: The other publication to which Lyris refers was *The Academy Journal*; in March 1961 her poem appeared in print there.

On May 2, 1961, De Stephano sent his apologies and said that the poem would be reprinted as corrected. He hoped that they could have a pleasant association even after a bad start. In October 1961 *Poetry Digest* went out of business.

Lyris prepared the following explanation of her poem **Bookshelf Bibelots** which was found in rough draft among her notes.

> *On the bookshelf in my room I have a number of objects which I prize. They include a small bowl of olive wood, some very old brass scales for weighing letters, and seven stones rounded into large pebbles by the action of a New England brook or glacier.*
>
> *I ask myself what these objects have represented to me; why I—who usually dislike dead souvenirs and have not made a fetish of them—see these on my bookshelf as healthful and sound. Upon reflection, I find a possible answer.*
>
> *Maybe the good which the olive tree (A. 4013[2]) represents may still be useful. The grey-eyed goddess of wisdom, Athene, gave the olive tree to the city which was named for her. Maybe the truth which the stones represent will somehow slay the Goliath of self-pride (F. 52e, T.276[2]), and therefore provide salvation. She who owns and cherishes these representative objects considers their value. She admits regretfully that she is neither wise like Athene nor brave like David.*
>
> *The wooden bowl and the stones, if there are even as many as five—the number which David had in his scrip, and signifying what is relatively little (A. 2576[6])—should be of equal importance as good and truth are. If we have at least some truth conjoined with good, it will endure.*
>
> *The truths of the Ancient Church represented by Greek mythology and the truths of the Old Testament are from the same source and will last for ages of ages.*

34

Bookshelf Bibelots

A lidded bowl of olive wood
A dull brass heirloom postal scale
And seven river-rounded stones....

For what have they stood
That I, who loathe dry dusty bones
Nor call them sacred, see these hale?

Perhaps the tree may still do good
That grey-eyed virgin goddess gave,
The pebbles from the brook not fail
And, giant-slaying somehow, save.
Their hoarder weighs their worth and owns,
Regretful, she's not wise or brave.

The olive gift, the stones (if there be five)
Have equal weight, or should, and will survive.

October 1958

Late in the summer of 1961 Lyris requested membership in the Poetry Society of America (PSA), perhaps because a few of her poems had been published and she had gained some confidence in her ability as a poet. Part of the membership requirement was to submit five poems for appraisal. Three of the poems she chose were: **Bright and Dark, To Live at Home,** and **Bookshelf Bibelots**; the last two were: **Set for Snow** and **Two Aunts and the Two-year-old.**

In October 1961 Lyris was accepted as a member of the PSA.

Set for Snow was written just after Christmas in 1958 when there had been no snowfall yet and the world was waiting for the first whiteness of the winter.

Louise Murray, a friend, to whom Lyris had sent several of her poems for comment, wrote about them:

> *Your poems have something of value to say and you say it with a light, quick touch. It reminds me of Emily Dickinson.*

Lyris was, of course, a great admirer of Emily Dickinson. She made an extensive study of her poems for a paper she wrote at Bread Loaf. Several of Lyris's poems show evidence of the cryptic Dickinson style, some of them even more than **Set for Snow.**

35

Set for Snow

The smell and feel of snow are in the air;
The ground is ready for it, hard and bare
And seeming all but dead. Impassiveness
Can be the mask for love as well as dread,
Some know. O laden clouds, be not misled.

December 31, 1958
Printed in *The Bread Loaf Poets* August 1961

The next poem, **Two Aunts and the Two-year-old** (one of the five submitted to the PSA), was written two years earlier at Bread Loaf in 1959 while Lyris was taking a writing course with William Meredith. The note is hers and was attached to the poem when she handed it in to the teacher for criticism.

> *Hyatt 17*
>
> *You called form a crutch, and I know what you mean. In this "Two Aunts" effort the form was more like a litter since the patient wasn't even ambulatory. I wrote the first three lines and was scared to death because, although I had thought about the subject for months, I felt all at loose ends and could not go on until I arbitrarily decided to find a rhyme for wants, and then committed myself to the tercet (?), which seemed both formal and informal. Sonya Utterback says the 8th stanza is not clear.* I want it to be and will change it if it seems unclear to you. Is the last line too corny? Clinton's father calls me Auntie Dote.*
>
> **Line 21 was part of her trouble.*

The rhyme scheme is really quite amazing, the form a difficult one and hard to sustain. The three-line stanzas and the interwoven rhymes give the poem a merry-go-round or ring-around-the-rosy pattern that suits the subject—an active, exploratory two-year-old with the aunts, Lyris and her sister Morna, dancing attendance.

36

Two Aunts and the Two-year-old

His third-floor aunts provide for all his wants
above the normal tender loving care
he gets at home: big beds to bounce or turn

fish-teeming ocean where he swims and pants
to reach the comfort of spread beach to air
his views on lotion for his hands, concern

for brushing teeth with paste, window sill plants
that need a lot of water brought from where
the stand-on scale and shower are. He'll spurn,

politely, help with finding the rag, but grants
he knows that overflows on floor, though rare,
are really careless and certainly he'll learn

how not to spill. Under the circumstance
he thinks it prudent now to ask for a chair
and room at the desk to crayon, or tries to earn

encouragement to look at books or dance
to FM symphony. Sometimes he'll stare
at something far away and won't return

until the fairyland which now enchants
him keeps him proof enough from auntly glare.
He too well knows his charms and can discern

that if he'd hear the music box, his chance
is now; that both of us are but a pair
of suckers for Vienna Waltz and yearn

to give him anything he wants. Soft adamants,
we see he's growing up, aware, away; and burn
to know what will be antidotes for doting aunts.

July 1959

At Heaven's Gate has 14 lines, but is not a true sonnet as the line length is short several syllables in most places. However, anyone familiar with Shakespeare's Sonnet #29 will find several allusions to that poem, and see how cleverly Lyris has used them to suit her own meaning.

37
At Heaven's Gate

I used to think I was content
With what I thought I most enjoyed;
I toyed with pun and complex rhyme
And played with cynic words half bent
To say at least a part of what
I thought I'd want to think they meant,
A kind of crossword scarecrow game
In skeletonic black and white,
Scarcely artless; heartless, smart,
Too light to matter much, and too much art.

O now I'd scorn to change my lot
    with anyone, forego all long-dreamed fame,
If I could find an honest line
    to mean as much to me as your dear name.

October 1, 1958

Apheliotropes means those who shun or turn away from the sun.

Lyris, because of her pale skin and red hair, couldn't take exposure to the sun. When chaperoning club or class shore trips or visiting a friend with an ocean-front house, she would never appear on the beach unless covered from ankle to wrist, a broad-brimmed hat tied under her chin, and a parasol. She certainly looked different from all the sun-worshippers around her; and her appearance often excited comments, usually well-meant. Lyris tried to be a good sport about her "defect," but this poem explains how she felt.

38

Apheliotropes

We thin-skinned fear a social seashore trip,
For sportsmanship and human decency
Insist we lie about the beach, agree
It's fun, stretched out in noonday sun, to strip
Ourselves, if not of long-sleeved shirt and slacks,
Of some reserve at least. We'd like to hide
Behind our magazines awhile, unfried,
Ungrilled by sun or friends, and just relax.

The stuff that's proof against the sun direct
Or too kind questioning can't yet be bought.
If we uncover face or mind too soon
We lose them both. Of course it's our defect
We feel we have to save ourselves; we ought
Not burn when well-meant warmth is merely importune.

November 6, 1958

Orientation is a superb poem. It says much, most concisely, and the rhymes are fresh and unusual. At first reading there may be some difficulty with the technical words, but a few minutes with the dictionary will add delight and depth to an understanding of the poem.

There is a lot to think about in a few lines—a truly New Church statement of faith.

39

Orientation

With centers two, antipodal,
The natural man is all at odds,
To his own will centripetal,
Centrifugal from what is God's.

Petitioner and fugitive,
He turns from ego's mad career
To lose himself at last and live
Secure in heaven-ordered sphere.

May 11, 1959
Published in *N.C.Education* June 1959

Poet Poses is a poem about writing poetry and the value of art compared to life. Most poets write at least one poem about writing. As well as this poem there are also lines in other poems which show that Lyris had the art of poesy on her mind. See **At Heaven's Gate** as she suggests.

It is interesting to read **Poet Poses** in the light of excerpts from a short paper written at Bread Loaf in 1959 for Mr. Meredith.

> *I'd like to be able to write poems based on New Church ("Swedenborgian") doctrine and philosophy but, foolishly or not, I'd want something of an audience, and probably not more than three or four people in the world have both the background of belief and the knowledgeable interest in poetry which would make them bother to read.*
>
> *All my efforts seem to say pretty much the same thing, which is tiresome. And they all start from words (except one which started with concrete objects, and one for which I assigned myself a subject which I thought would be difficult). Most are a sort of word puzzle and patchwork of various kinds of echoes and seem to need more action, music, and richness; too artsy-crafty (see* "At Heaven's Gate"*). Paradoxically, I would like to be in control of the words rather than being in theirs. They often perversely have their own way and I can't quite get them back on the track I began to intend. The only critic that I have had says that I should work on maintaining and developing my own "voice," but I don't know what it is, or else don't like what I suspect it is. . . .*
>
> *If I have one virtue in the writing line, I suppose it is that I spend a lot of paper, time, and work on what I do; but this doesn't make up for the rush of emotion and ideas which I wish I had so that I could have the pleasure of reducing them to some satisfactory form.*

40

Poet Poses

Write when you're angry, you advise,
Slash half your lines and tauten those
You spare. But something soundly shies
From such advice. I should suppose
Your stringent words would rouse me; wise
Or wild ones used to. Now I close
My mind and try to rationalize
This lack of action: Life is prose,
And one who merely versifies
Is helpless, hopeless; Goodness knows
That poetasters in the guise
Of poets *ought* to decompose.

What lies one writes when the lines comprise
No more than verbal furbelows!

April 3, 1960

Dead Weight relates to **Bookshelf Biblelots** in that the poet is using the same stones in both poems. A painter will often paint again and again some material objects in his studio that have special meaning, even though the value of the object in each work of art may be very different.

In a letter to Jonathan Aldrich, April 1959, Lyris mentions the stones as ones "I picked up around Bread Loaf for possible paperweights." This is the way of a symbol. It begins as something natural, material, even practical, and acquires meaning on another plane according to the artist's imagination.

41

Dead Weight

These stones weight paper, prop my book,
And on occasion stop my door.

But the one you dropped that night in the water,
No matter how the circles spread,
    Is a weight more dead,
    Now all is said,
    Than these on my desk
        And floor.

July 21, 1961
Revised March 30, 1962

The only copy of **Never Before a Fall** in Lyris's file of poems is mimeographed, which suggests that she used it as an exercise with one of her classes. Now, it is considered useful for the teacher of writing to do the same assignments as the students, but Lyris was ahead of the pedagogical practice of her day in sharing her poems with the girls and allowing them to criticize her work as a way of improving their own.

This poem is not included on Lyris's master list of her poems; it is undated; there is a large penciled X on top of the page and many little X's down the stanzas. Several words crossed out or changed also suggest that she didn't like it much or wasn't yet satisfied with it. At the risk of offending her the poem is included here because the editor liked it.

42

Never Before a Fall

Seldom a day—a part of a day—
Like this; and never before a fall.
I'm sitting here in a field by a wall,
The stones warm and the same pale grey

As the lace of leafless trees beyond
This open field. A chickadee
With not a hint of mystery
Is practicing close by the pond

Far down the slope. Unmoved, the hills
Lie quiet under a pristine sky
With only a wisp of a cloud high
In the west. The air moves now and spills

Out leaves like birds, and birds like leaves
Scud by above unfaded asters.
One butterfly fears no disasters;
One tree's live gold is all reprieves.

This piece of world this year is clear and free,
None of its colors muddled or muddied by me.

Like **Never Before a Fall, Winter Beech** shows the poet's affection for the Lord's creation and a keen, observing eye.

Lyris reworked this poem several times. I chose the latest version and the one I liked best. Notice how different in style it is from most of her earlier poems. Perhaps this was the result of the writing course which she took with the poet John Frederick Nims. His influence on her writing was quite different from that of her earlier teacher, William Meredith.

43

Winter Beech

Roots splayed
clutch the sodden bank
splotched with shrunken snow
to brace the grey suede trunk
half in amethyst shadow
below silver branches
that tangle and reach,
feathering into lace,
tracery against pale porcelain
faint blue, stained rose
and jade.

And now, look where
that one small bird is: there.

July 31, 1965

Not Easy, although somewhat introspective and personal, still speaks to the universal condition. In comparing ourselves to others how often we see ourselves as falling short.

The structure of the poem is off balance in that the first line of each stanza is longer that the other three. Yet the pattern of each stanza is the same and the rhyme scheme tight. Here the form strengthens the concept. For rigidity can arise from the lack of self-confidence and awkwardness from inhibition.

44

Not Easy

Poised, light-footed, cool
in gesture, word;
never the fool,
never absurd,

how easily you move.
Apparently
you need no groove.
Who set you free?

How can you be so sure
of No and Yes—
What is the cure
for awkwardness?

1965

Emendation has a flavor of Frost about it—economy coupled with the conversational tone.

The poet is self-conscious, yet saved from taking herself too seriously by the touch of whimsy. It's as if she were cocking an eyebrow at her own shortcomings rather than wringing her hands.

45

Emendation

A stitch in time may well save nine,
But stitches needed in things of mine
Are never single. I contend
It's almost always too late to mend.

Written 1958
Revised 1966

In a letter to her friend Jonathan Aldrich, Lyris wrote:

How wonderful that you have been working and that your work got recognized in a clearly recognizable way. I'm very happy for you and couldn't put off telling you so nor thanking you for the sunny picture and especially for the citation. I'm glad to take any credit given for encouragement, but surely you wouldn't have stopped writing no matter what. Anyway, thanks a lot, and do send at least one of the poems even if I am dense.

Thanks too for your minatory advice. It helps, but I always want to work—would like nothing—well almost nothing—better, but I am committed to my job, and whether you believe it or not it takes a lot of time and poetry can be just an escape. I get to scribbling and crossing out and lose all track of time. Some weeks ago I decided that a poem about spring would be the hardest thing to do that I could think of. The result was the enclosed, which is just about as literate as I could make it. Any religious overtones should be discounted about 98%. If they are there, it is only the result of the name of the flowers. It's just my temperamental sympathy for the long haul as against the martyr or flashy heroism.

The poem Lyris refers to here is **Synonymies of Spring** which she first wrote in 1959.

In 1965 Lyris revised the poem and showed it to Donald Davidson, an instructor at Bread Loaf that summer. Mr. Davidson thought well of the poem and suggested that Lyris send it to the *Georgia Review*, a quarterly magazine edited by his brother Wallace Davidson.

The poem was submitted, accepted, and published, and Lyris received $7.00 in payment—the first and only money she got for a poem.

I think this is the best poem I ever wrote as far as sounds are concerned, she once noted.

And further:

(I do like robins if I see them in February as martyrs, and I love the silver maple buds bright red against the sky.) But realness to me is the Star-of-Bethlehem bulbs in the gutter between our place and Mr. Cole's. The flowers do bloom anywhere from the 16th to the 18th of May. The theory I have held for several years is that if the poet does an honest job, he (she?) will get a dividend. I think I did in this piece.

46

Synonymies of Spring

Not your robin in February,
huddled glum on the apple branch,
nor blood-red buds of the silver maple
swelling gallant in a blue March sky;

but in the gutter, dry or sodden,
almost hidden in the gravel,
here, these pearl-size ivory bulbs,
through all the rains or drought of April,
put up with it. They wait it out.

To startle a morning,
from them will stem
six petals, white
and subtle, bright:
the mid-May Star-of-Bethlehem.

March 13, 1959
Revised drastically July 1965

47

Recital Number from Book Two
(5/4 measure)

Our child world is twice dear.
Then space-time was not mere
but here, now, and all right
through real noon and good night.

The black storm or slammed door
was no less yet no more
than dark fact or safe end
of one phase or one friend.

But now old, and less wise
in some ways, the heart sighs
its half-truths in singsong:
the past's all—or all wrong.

August 1960
Printed in *Bread Loaf Poets*

A Song and **Recital Number** are two versions of a poem which underwent a number of revisions over the years with a number of titles: "No More," "Degree of Declination," "Sing Song," among others. The 1973 version, **A Song,** has several of Lyris's comments in the margins which have been included here.

It is interesting to note that, although the versions are basically the same until the last line, the final line makes a big difference as does the form.

48

A Song

Unfinished and not yet abandoned

Our child world   is twice dear
Then space time   spelled no fear
The here now   was all right
through real noon   to good night

The black storm   the slammed door
were no less   yet no more
than dark fact   or safe end
of this phase   of that friend

Now no child   and less wise
in some ways   my heart sighs
its half-truths   in singsong:
Life's short   Art's long.

1973

Annotation can be a gossipy intrusion

I had written the first draft of this some fifteen years ago

*I was amazed to realize that the meter was that of the clock in the nursery (!) * of my grandmother's house. I was born in this house, and despite the disbelief of others I maintain memory of the nursery at a year and a half.*

*Nursery *is in my reading vocabulary, but I never say it!*

Another of Lyris's favorite poets was Gerard Manley Hopkins, a Jesuit priest who wrote fervent religious poetry. This fragment is certainly written in an attempt to put into a Hopkins framework her own response to the Lord's creation. Hopkins wrote: *Glory be to God for dappled things.* Lyris wrote: *Glory be to God for order, form—*

49

Glory be to God for order, form—
    for planets round their suns; for daisy petals
        like lashes round the sunny eye of day;
For cycles; the eye at the center of the wheeling storm;
    for all that rises or ferments; for all that settles
        in its own time and sphere in its own way;
Everything measured, symmetrical, framed, enclosed;
    whatever has tension, rhythm, focus, poise;
All things composing because they have been composed
    by One who intends, provides, and informs my joys.

1967

There is no evidence that Lyris wrote much poetry in her later years, at least not much that she felt was ready to type up in a finished form. In the back of her ordered file of poems are a number of penciled manuscripts obviously still in the process of formation. As they are not dated there is no way of knowing when she was working on them. But in a way no poem is ever dated. It holds for its moment all that the poet understands and loves; all that was and is, and future hopes and dreams too.

This one across the page does all of that. And its unfinished state reminds us that our life is never finished even though the years on earth come to an end.

In the Resurrection Address for Lyris delivered December 10th 1986 the Rev. Kurt Asplundh said:

> *Her hopes for marriage can now be fulfilled. We are told in the Heavenly Doctrine about "those who in the state, have desired marriage, and still more . . . those who have solicited it without success." "For them, if they are spiritual, blessed marriages are provided. . ."* (CL 54, 229).
>
> *It is delightful to think that the Lord, in His Providence, will soon provide this opportunity of marriage for not one, but two who have longed for its blessings throughout life. Perhaps as it is for those who grow up in the heavens, a meeting will take place, as if by chance, where that wonderful recognition will occur, "He is mine." "She is mine."* (CL 229).
>
> *Lyris will bring to her marriage a depth of affection and sensitivity to others that she has developed during her life on earth. We carry our character and loves to the spiritual world intact. As a member of a large and unique family with strong roots in the New church, as a teacher and observer of human nature, she has become prepared for heavenly uses in a special way. She has labored in language and life to craft what was beautiful, appropriate and right, and has known both success and failure. Now, if it is her will, she can enter into heavenly uses without the limitations of this world to mar or inhibit her efforts.*

I looked to see you come,
Certain that you would
If I would just keep dumb
~~And seek the true and good~~
Remembering to be good.
But then you did not come
And I did what I could
I snatched at every crumb
Until I understood.
~~I'll wait to find you now~~
~~Much later than I'd thought~~
~~That I must wait awhile~~
~~And change myself to one~~
And now the fever's past,
The search postponed a while.
In ~~other realm~~ at last
I'll know your knowing smile

And I'm content to wait
~~Till~~ For hand in hand at last